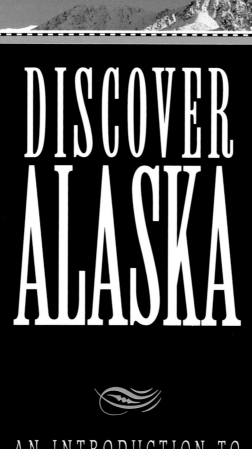

DISCOVER ALASKA

AN INTRODUCTION TO AMERICA'S LAST FRONTIER

Alaska Northwest Books

Anchorage • Seattle

Library of Congress Cataloging-in-Publication Data
Discover Alaska: an introduction to America's last frontier.
        p.   cm.
  Includes bibliographical references and index.
  ISBN 0-88240-412-1
    1. Alaska—Description and travel—1981-
F910.5.D57   1991
979.8—dc20   91-31722
                                                 CIP

Edited by Anne Halloran
Book, cover design and maps by Kate L. Thompson
Photography supplied by West Stock, Inc., Seattle, Washington

Front cover: Sunset on Glacier Bay, Southeast Alaska.
Back cover: Tlingit totem pole among Sitka spruce, Sitka National Historical Park.
Half-title page: Walrus on the beach at Walrus Islands Game Sanctuary, Bristol Bay.
Frontispiece: The Chugach Mountains rise east of Anchorage.

Photo credits: William Boehm, page 37; Tom Collicott, 49; Alissa Crandall, 5(left), 51,
52(bottom); Terry Domico, 56; Dennis Doran, 57; David Falconer, 41, 46(top); Jane Gnass, 21,
24(top); Jeff Gnass, front cover, back cover, 6, 13, 15, 16, 19, 42, 58, 59; Michael Graber, 38; Keith
Gunnar, 44; Lon E. Lauber, 5(top), 17(bottom); Tom and Pat Leeson, 5(bottom), 17(top), 25;
Mark Newman, 1, 26-27, 27(top), 39, 53, 55; Don Normark, 50; M. Timothy O'Keefe, 31, 36; Allen
Prier, 2-3, 10-11, 22-23, 32-33; John W.Warden, 29(top), 29(bottom), 33, 34, 52; Don Wilson, 47.

Alaska Northwest Books™
A division of GTE Discovery Publications, Inc.
22026 20th Avenue S.E.
Bothell, Washington 98021

Printed in Singapore

Contents

Foreword *by Art Davidson*   7

DISCOVER THE NORTH COUNTRY   10

SOUTHEAST
The Kingdom of the Raven   13

SOUTHCENTRAL/GULF COAST
The Golden Door   21

THE INTERIOR
The Heart of the Country   31

ALASKA PENINSULA/
ALEUTIAN ISLANDS
The Land of Smoky Seas   41

THE BERING SEA COAST
The Bridge to Long Ago   49

THE ARCTIC
A Timeless World of White   55

Recommended Reading   60
Index   61

CLOCKWISE FROM BOTTOM LEFT:
VISITORS EXPLORE TLINGIT
COMMUNITY HOUSE IN
KETCHIKAN. BALD EAGLE IN
FLIGHT. CANOERS ON WONDER
LAKE WITH MOUNT MCKINLEY
IN THE BACKGROUND.

Foreword

Alaska is often called the last frontier. But it's no longer a frontier in the way we imagine the Old West—untracked and lawless, with wild creatures everywhere. Alaska has towns with street lights and shopping malls. Still, Alaska remains out there at the edge where civilization and wilderness meet. Polar bears wander in from the pack ice. Natives go out to hunt, much as their ancestors did centuries ago. In a world in which indigenous people, wildlife, and wild places are rapidly disappearing, Alaska can help us find or reaffirm our relationship to nature. And it has a way of bringing out the explorer in us.

When I came to Alaska in the 1960s, I was drawn to unclimbed peaks and glaciers where no one had ever walked. But Alaska's wildness is also close at hand—moose wander city streets and grizzlies browse for berries within sight of town. You can feel the pulse of wild Alaska in flocks of geese and swans that fill the skies of spring. There are primal stirrings in the sea: the great whales rise and dive, and salmon fight tides and currents to spawn a thousand miles up river. If you are lucky, you might see a wolf following caribou on their way north to calve on the Arctic coastal plain.

In a sense, we are all visitors to this frontier. Whether we explore Alaska for a week or a lifetime, each of us can experience its natural grandeur and get to know some of its people. It's my hope that along the way we can also discover ways to safeguard and perpetuate the wildness that makes Alaska so precious, so irreplaceable.

LEFT: CARIBOU ANTLERS LIE ON THE TUNDRA BENEATH THE BROOKS RANGE, NORTH OF THE ARCTIC CIRCLE.

—Art Davidson, author of *In the Wake of the EXXON VALDEZ* and *Circle of Light*

Discover the North Country

ho has not dreamed of the Last Frontier, of towering
mountains, pristine vistas, and wild, untrammeled space?
Those fortunate enough to visit Alaska know it does not
disappoint. Superlatives rightly tumble from the traveler's
mouth, shaping images of vastness and invulnerability. But
there is another story. The land of the polar bear is the realm
of the fragile tundra flower.

For centuries, Alaska has symbolized not only unsurpassed
beauty but inexhaustible bounty, and both qualities have
drawn the outsider. The first tourists ventured across the
Bering Sea Land Bridge many thousands of years ago,
migrating from Asia to the upper reaches of the Arctic.
Nineteenth-century explorers and surveyors carted measuring
tools: how high did its craggy peaks soar, and how widespread
are its crystalline lakes? Even those who came for riches
departed with visions, opening the land for settlement by
others. The fur trader and gold seeker paved the way for the
schoolteacher and farmer. From earliest times, another

ABOVE: FLOATPLANES RIM LAKE
HOOD IN ANCHORAGE, THE
LARGEST SEAPLANE BASE IN THE
WORLD.

message emerged, one of love for Alaska's unique landscape. Georg Steller, the botanist who accompanied Vitus Bering on his 1741 Arctic voyage, named new species and plants and cautioned against exploitation. Naturalist John Muir's late nineteenth-century accounts of Southeast's glaciers remain stirring invocations of the land's power.

Alaska's majesty continues to inspire succeeding generations of explorers. They come to test themselves among its formidable mountain ranges, to learn from its complex peoples, and to admire geography unlike any elsewhere on earth. The northern lights still ignite the sky. Massive glacier seracs separate without warning, exploding into the sea. Eskimo masks reveal a Native culture of depth and richness. Herds of caribou thunder across the tundra in a graceful sweep. These encounters and untold others create impressions that endure. The experience of Alaska awaits the casual visitor as well as the serious student of the Arctic. Alaska is the source of endless discovery.

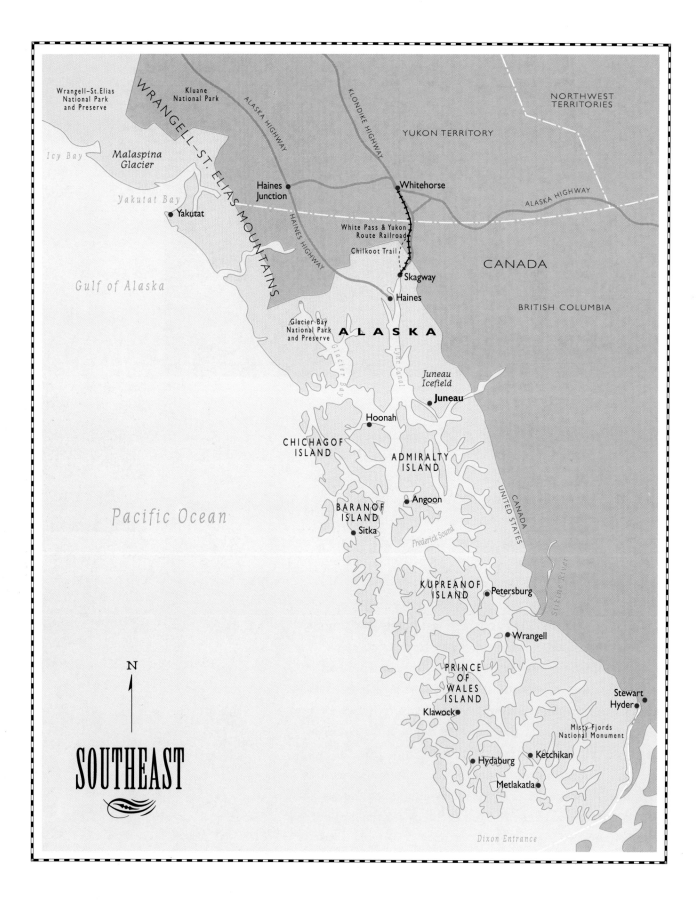

Wrangell–St. Elias
National Park
and Preserve

Kluane
National Park

ALASKA HIGHWAY

KLONDIKE HIGHWAY

NORTHWEST
TERRITORIES

YUKON TERRITORY

Icy Bay

Malaspina
Glacier

WRANGELL–ST. ELIAS MOUNTAINS

Haines
Junction

Whitehorse

ALASKA HIGHWAY

Yakutat Bay

Yakutat

HAINES HIGHWAY

White Pass & Yukon
Route Railroad

Chilkoot Trail

CANADA

Gulf of Alaska

Skagway

Haines

BRITISH COLUMBIA

Glacier Bay
National Park
and Preserve

ALASKA

Lynn Canal

Juneau
Icefield

Glacier Bay

Juneau

Hoonah

CHICHAGOF
ISLAND

ADMIRALTY
ISLAND

Pacific Ocean

BARANOF
ISLAND

Angoon

UNITED STATES

CANADA

Sitka

Frederick Sound

Stikine River

KUPREANOF
ISLAND

Petersburg

Wrangell

N

PRINCE
OF
WALES
ISLAND

Stewart
Hyder

Klawock

Misty Fjords
National Monument

SOUTHEAST

Hydaburg

Ketchikan

Metlakatla

Dixon Entrance

The Kingdom of the Raven

*Tracing shining ways
through fjords and
sounds, past forests and
waterfalls, islands and
mountains and far azure
headlands, it seems
surely we must at length
reach the very paradise
of the poets, the abode of
the blessed.*

*–John Muir
  Travels in Alaska, 1879*

Totems rise from shrouds of mist, like phantoms on the Pacific Northwest Coast. Monuments in cedar, these poles tell the ancient stories of their creators, the indigenous Native peoples, and are steeped in myth. Along the Inside Passage, the carvings call out to the traveler, signaling entrance to a land of supernatural beauty.

The Inside Passage is a protected coastal waterway extending from Seattle, Washington, to Skagway, Alaska. As the 1,000-mile route moves north to Southeast Alaska, wonders mount. Countless islands, the steep-sided tops of a long-submerged mountain range, break through the surface of the water. Glaciers preside over deep channels like immense prows, surrounded by snowcapped peaks. Fjord, inlet, and bay interweave in a maritime mosaic.

The waters of the northern Inside Passage teem with marine mammals, including porpoises, Steller sea lions, and harbor seals. The high dorsal fins of orcas (killer whales) slice through the waves with a swift grace. Humpback whales migrate here from Mexico and Hawaii each summer, occasionally surprising onlookers with a breach. Hurtling into the air for a glorious moment, the whale's huge body

RIGHT: A CONTEMPORARY
TLINGIT TOTEM POLE IN
DOWNTOWN JUNEAU.

fills the sky, then falls back into the sea with a thunderous crash.

One-half of the passage lies within Southeast Alaska, a region known as the Panhandle. The waterway is a lifeline to the 50,000 people who live beside it, most clustered in a handful of settlements. For great distances, signs of civilization are few, limited to the sporadic blinking of remote lighthouses.

Panhandle cities are some of Alaska's oldest, and residents cherish their colorful histories. Now the state's sophisticated capital, Juneau originated in a gold-flushed frenzy. Petersburg honors its Scandinavian heritage with the annual Little Norway Festival. Wrangell, situated on the Stikine River as well as the Inside Passage, has existed under three flags—British, Russian, and American. The traditional artistry of local Natives is displayed at Ketchikan's Totem Heritage Center, the state's largest collection of totem poles. All along the Inside Passage, modern buildings meet touches of the rustic past. Cedar-plank streets and houses poised on pilings look out upon the still beauty of the waterway.

Only in the uppermost reaches of the Panhandle do roads carry people to points Outside. The rest of Southeast's residents rely on airplanes and boats for transportation. Ferries of the Alaska Marine Highway System and cruise ships travel numerous routes.

A network of channels connects islands in the passage to the mainland. All manner of life thrives in this lush world. Southeast's combination of mild temperatures and heavy rains produces luxuriance: woods are dense, and lichen, deep moss, and ferns flourish beneath the trees. Old-growth forests cloak the region in an almost impenetrable blanket of green. Toward the north, the Douglas firs prevalent in British Columbia gradually give way, yielding to stands of hemlock, Sitka spruce, and cedar. Seventy-five percent of Southeast Alaska is encompassed in the Tongass National Forest. Established by President Theodore Roosevelt early in the century, the Tongass is the country's biggest national forest, consisting of almost 16.8 million acres. A recreational haven for campers, hikers, hunters, and anglers, the Tongass is also a lure for loggers and miners. Pressure is great to satisfy competing demands on the forest's precious resources.

Animals are also prolific throughout Southeast Alaska. Sitka blacktail deer, mountain goats, lynx, wolverine, and river otter

abound. Over 1,000 Alaska brown bears—coastal grizzlies—live on Admiralty Island. Nourished by a rich diet of vegetation, berries, and migrating salmon, the bears grow unusually large, some to 1,500 pounds. Millions of waterfowl, including exotic auklets and horned and tufted puffins, nest in Southeast sea-cliff rookeries. Fish and shellfish fill area waters. Pacific salmon return here, fighting to spawn up freshwater rivers. Halibut, herring, black cod, and pollock swim in the cold, deep bays.

In the forests, ravens cry out, as they have for thousands of years. Bald eagles, more plentiful in the Chilkat River Valley than anywhere else on earth, feed along the rivers and inlets. Both the raven and the eagle are revered by coastal Natives, for whom they represent wisdom and experience. Legends about the raven are told and retold, preserving a heritage and gently guiding the steps of the young.

Many Southeast Natives are Indian, one of three separate ethnic and linguistic groups that first inhabited Alaska. The other groups are the Eskimos (including the Inupiat and Yupik), who historically occupied the coastline from the Arctic Ocean to Yakutat Bay, and the Aleuts, who originally lived on the Aleutian Islands. Among Alaskan Indians are the Athapaskans of the Interior, and the coastal Indians—the Haida, Tsimshian, and Tlingit—who share similar histories and traditions.

Artistic and powerful, the Tlingit embraced all that was around them. The region's richness made possible a culture of breadth and beauty. Even simple domestic items were embellished with intricate carvings and brightly painted designs. A cornerstone of Tlingit life was the potlatch, a celebration full of ritual and gift-giving. To acquire their wealth, the Tlingit became ardent traders, traveling as far south as Puget Sound in their long dugout canoes. Spiritual expressions were also cherished by the Indians, who created a deep reservoir of stories, dances, and songs.

Natives make up 20 percent of the population in Southeast, and reside both in larger towns and smaller communities such as Hoonah, Hydaburg, and Klawock.

Russian settlement in Alaska started after the explorations of Vitus Bering in 1741. A Dane in the service of the Czar Peter, Bering is credited with leading the first European expedition to Alaska. Members of the group returned to Russia with sea otter

Icebergs shimmer in the twilight beneath Mendenhall Glacier, just outside of Juneau.

pelts, intensifying the region's mystique. Several decades later, men from British captain James Cook's voyages also brought furs to an admiring world. These accounts and others unleashed a torrent of traders.

While the powerful Hudson's Bay Company had outposts throughout the continent's inland areas, the Russian-American Company, a monopoly licensed by the czar, dominated Alaska. From their headquarters of New Archangel, later renamed Sitka, Russians like Alexander Baranov wielded enormous influence for almost 70 years. The indefatigable Baranov sought to recreate the pomp of the Old World's St. Petersburg with a palatial residence and onion-domed buildings. That era survives in modern-day Sitka, where Byzantine spires still pierce the skyline. The Sitka National Historic Fort and Sheldon Jackson College and Museum are among the places where visitors can brush close to the past. Saint Michael's Russian Orthodox Cathedral glows with gold leaf, stained glass, and jeweled icons.

The Russian period officially ended in 1867, when Alaska was sold to the United States (the sale took place even though the

TOP: Killer whales are distinguished by high dorsal fins.

ABOVE: The imperious bald eagle.

Russians never held any title to the region). At the time, most Americans believed the distant acquisition was a waste of money. They mocked the sale and the secretary of state who engineered it by calling Alaska "Seward's Folly." Within a few decades, Southeast Alaska's bounty proved the wisdom of the trade. By 1912, one-half billion dollars in silver, copper, coal, fisheries, and furs was taken out. Perhaps no finding excited as much attention as gold. The first strike took place on the upper Stikine River near Wrangell in 1861, and others followed in Windham Bay and Baranof Island. In Juneau, an unusually rich pocket of gold-bearing quartz created a momentum that lasted for years.

Lured by the prospect of instant wealth, fortune seekers hastened to the region. Southeast towns such as Skagway and Dyea became portals to the gold fields, their populations multiplying overnight. Stampeders made arduous treks up steep mountain passes, pictures of grim determination. After the turn of the century, the White Pass & Yukon Route tamed the most treacherous route of all, from Skagway to Whitehorse. Hikers can recreate the journey today. Skagway's Klondike Gold Rush National Historical Park includes the 33-mile-long Chilkoot Trail, the miners' path over the Chilkoot Pass to Lake Bennett. And the old narrow-gauge railroad still exists, providing thrilling rides out of Skagway over White Pass.

Skagway is the end of the Inside Passage, but many people disembark in Haines, where they can travel by highway to other parts of Alaska. Founded as a Presbyterian mission in 1881, picturesque Haines is surrounded by mountains. Nearby Lynn Canal and Chilkoot and Chilkat inlets furnish plenty of salmon.

While the heady days of the gold rush have passed, nature's spectacles have generated a new breed of prospector—the tourist. Perhaps the most magnificent attraction is the glacier, the land's architect. These icy chisels once shaped the whole of Southeast, sculpting narrow coastal valleys, rugged bays, and steep-walled fjords. Despite their quiescent beauty, glaciers pose the constant threat of sudden fury. The lore of ancient peoples recounts how massive icebergs roared to life without warning, engulfing whole villages.

Glaciers can never be domesticated, but in Southeast, many no longer encroach. Some are even retreating, hanging from steep mountainsides, beckoning the curious for a closer look at

their eerie blue walls. The most accessible is Mendenhall Glacier, part of the Juneau Ice Fields and a short trip from the city's center.

In Glacier Bay National Park and Preserve, 16 active tidewater glaciers form a living ice age. When British explorer George Vancouver sailed past the bay in 1794, it was barely a dent in the coastline. Since then, the glaciers have retreated 65 miles, leaving a labyrinth of deep fjords. The movement of the icebergs continues. They calve and crash and drift in endless sequence. To naturalist John Muir, the process is simply the world remaking itself: "Out of all the cold darkness and glacial crushing comes this warm, abounding beauty and life to teach us that what we in our faithless ignorance and fear call destruction is creation finer and finer."

A CRUISE SHIP SAILS THROUGH GLACIER BAY AT SUNSET, PASSING A BREATHTAKING SWEEP OF TIDEWATER GLACIERS.

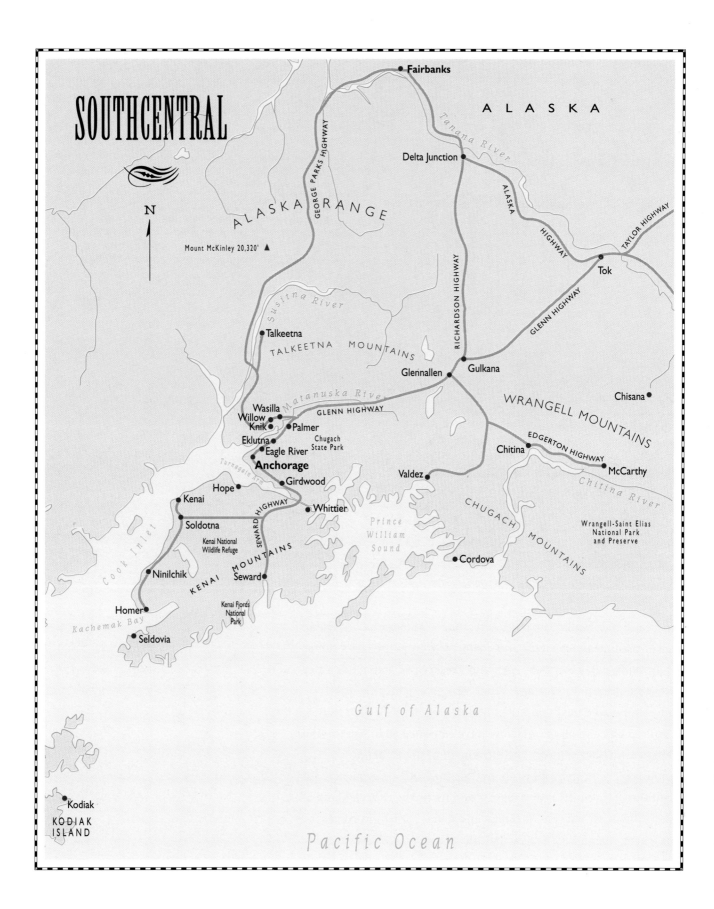

SOUTHCENTRAL

N

ALASKA

Mount McKinley 20,320' ▲

ALASKA RANGE

GEORGE PARKS HIGHWAY

Fairbanks

Tanana River

Delta Junction

ALASKA HIGHWAY

TAYLOR HIGHWAY

Tok

RICHARDSON HIGHWAY

GLENN HIGHWAY

Susitna River

Talkeetna

TALKEETNA MOUNTAINS

Glennallen

Gulkana

Chisana

WRANGELL MOUNTAINS

Matanuska River

Wasilla

Willow

Knik

Palmer

GLENN HIGHWAY

EDGERTON HIGHWAY

Eklutna

Eagle River

Chugach State Park

Chitina

McCarthy

Anchorage

Valdez

Chitina River

Turnagain Arm

Girdwood

Hope

Kenai

SEWARD HIGHWAY

Whittier

Prince William Sound

CHUGACH MOUNTAINS

Wrangell-Saint Elias National Park and Preserve

Soldotna

Kenai National Wildlife Refuge

KENAI MOUNTAINS

Cordova

Cook Inlet

Ninilchik

Seward

Homer

Kenai Fjords National Park

Kachemak Bay

Seldovia

Gulf of Alaska

Kodiak

KODIAK ISLAND

Pacific Ocean

The Golden Door

Not far from the center of Anchorage, a statue of Captain James Cook stands, turned toward the sea. Just as its namesake did in 1778, the figure seems to be searching the water, intently seeking an answer there. Preoccupied with finding the legendary passage between the Atlantic and Pacific oceans, the British explorer did not tarry along Alaska's Southcentral coast. The name Turnagain Arm, marking a sliver of water reaching southeast from Cook Inlet, bears witness to his frustration. Foiled by blustery winds, Cook would try to navigate Turnagain several times before sailing on to Hawaii.

Since those days, many others have followed in the path of the great mariner, but few departed disappointed. Over half of Alaska's more than 500,000 residents make their home in the diverse Southcentral region. The sea breathes warmth into much of this part of Alaska; mountains shelter it from arctic blasts and excessive rains. Nature smiles on the area in other ways as well, ringing its modern communities with a recreational paradise. Urban dwellers can quickly leave city life behind, spending weekends clamming on the Kenai Peninsula or kayaking through Prince William Sound.

AN ESKIMO SPIRIT CARVING ON DISPLAY AT THE WILLIAM EGAN CONVENTION CENTER IN ANCHORAGE.

SOUTHCENTRAL   21

Visitors to Southcentral Alaska will frequently stop first in
Anchorage. A tent camp prior to World War I, the settlement's
maturation into the state's largest city has not been without
struggle. Like the formidable tides of Cook Inlet—at more than 30
feet, their sweep is among the world's greatest—turbulence marks
Anchorage's history. While prosperity has favored the city on
many occasions, lean times have often followed close at its heels.
When Anchorage was named part of the Alaska Railroad route in
1915, job seekers streamed into the area, only to abandon it when
the work was completed. Construction of Air Force and Army
bases in the 1940s and 1950s funneled new wealth into the
economy. In 1964, North America's most severe earthquake
devastated the city. The 1970s saw a remarkable boom with the
creation of the trans-Alaska pipeline. Then, when oil prices
temporarily declined, so did the municipality's finances. But
occasional setbacks have not dimmed the spirit of this brash
young city, so splendidly pinned between the mountains and
the sea.

Those who journey to Anchorage anticipating a quiet sojourn
in an out-of-the-way hamlet will be surprised. The community is
a burgeoning center of commerce and transportation, a gateway
to the world's far corners. Like any metropolis, Anchorage
wrestles with the problems presented by skyscrapers, urban

spread, and congested freeways. But residents also enjoy
amenities such as a performing arts center, a zoo, two competing
daily newspapers, fine restaurants, and colorful nightclubs.

For all its modernity, Anchorage has one foot solidly planted
in the wilderness. The towering Chugach Mountains are visible
from throughout the city, and hikers can explore parts of the
heavily glaciated range in nearby Chugach State Park. In Ship
Creek on the edge of town, anglers catch huge king and silver
salmon. Wild geese and ducks nest aside busy streets. Evenings,
the silence of the hillsides may be broken by the soulful cry of a
wolf. And travelers hastening to busy Anchorage International
Airport may find themselves delayed by a moose standing
implacably on the highway.

Anchorage is also the jumping-off point for more ambitious
outdoor experiences. Numerous air taxi services are headquartered
near the city's Lake Hood Air Harbor, the world's largest
floatplane base. Bush pilots fly visitors to distant points, offering
once-in-a-lifetime glimpses of pristine landscapes. The number of
takeoffs from Anchorage's Merrill Field rivals the busiest
commercial airport in the Lower 48. Dependence on air travel is
one characteristic all Alaskans share; state per-capita ownership
of airplanes is the highest in the world.

Fortunately, access to an airplane isn't necessary to view

Southcentral's scenery. Large sections of the region are joined by roads. Within a day's drive of Anchorage are Seward, Palmer, and Valdez. Unique histories flavor these sites, and past cultures color their architecture and place names. The region's status as a crossroads is not recent. For some 10,000 years, the paths of Eskimo Natives and Athapaskan Indian groups entwined. All sought a share of Southcentral's plenitude. Two centuries ago, the Spanish and British arrived, desiring riches and shorter trade routes.

Many communities show evidence of the first European settlers, the Russian fur hunters. Along the northern edge of Knik Arm in the village of Eklutna, Russian traditions mingle with those of the Tanaina Indians. Eklutna is the site both of prehistoric Native trails and later trading posts. Forebears rest in a small cemetery, shadowed by a Russian Orthodox church. Tiny structures cover the graves, preserving the possessions of the dead. These bright "spirit houses" link the Tanainas' venerable culture to the faith they adopted.

Late in the nineteenth century, miners followed fur traders into Southcentral Alaska. Prospectors gave birth to rough-and-tumble towns, many of which still exist. Along Turnagain Arm, the settlement of Hope sprang from the muskeg after a series of minor gold rushes; today it is a tiny, tranquil retreat. Cordova blossomed as a shipping port for the Kennecott copper mines. Coal seams attracted interest near present-day Homer.

Agriculture added another chapter to the area's history. While its successes were never as dramatic as those of mining or oil, farming also shaped Southcentral in enduring ways. Agriculture tempted a different kind of newcomer, one whose dreams centered on forging a lasting bond with the land. During the Depression, 200 Midwestern families resettled in the Matanuska Valley north of Anchorage. Despite hardships, the farmers persevered, setting a new agricultural course in the state. They proved that all manner of crops could grow in Alaska, nurtured by fertile soil, cool temperatures, and long summer days. In the Matanuska Valley, fruits and vegetables may sprout to record size. As development diminishes the land available for farming, bucolic valley communities have regrouped, establishing new identities. Palmer is the seat of local government, and Wasilla a blossoming tourist center.

ABOVE: THIS EKLUTNA LOG SHRINE IS A REMINDER OF ITS RUSSIAN LEGACY.

RIGHT: A MOOSE SURPRISES A MOTORIST ON AN ALASKAN HIGHWAY.

GEORG STELLER

Not everyone came to Alaska to acquire. Remarkable exceptions to the fur traders and gold seekers were the explorers and scientists, who surmounted tremendous obstacles in their efforts to chart the wilderness. One such individual was Georg Steller, the German naturalist. Steller is generally considered to be the first European to set foot on Alaskan soil, going ashore on Kayak Island near present-day Cordova in 1741.

The brilliant Steller accompanied the second Vitus Bering expedition, and he was enthralled by the exotic flora and fauna he encountered. The Steller jay, Steller sea lion, and Steller eider are among the many species he documented and conscientiously described. Only his account survives of the sea cow, a mammal now forever gone from the sea. Steller's abilities to identify and classify were extraordinary, and he possessed a prodigious capacity to absorb detail. When he had no paper, he recorded his findings on crude sailcloth.

Steller was also trained as a physician. As the voyage progressed, he grew fearful the ship's crew would succumb to scurvy. Steller entreated Bering to stop for vitamin-rich plants and berries. But the expedition's leader was anxious to return to Russia. Within a few weeks, the vessel ran aground near what is now called Bering Island, and the captain and many others perished of scurvy.

Steller was among the few survivors of the expedition. Fashioning a crude boat, these men returned to the Russian mainland in 1742. Their accomplishments were soon forgotten. The observations of a scientist—one who cautioned against exploitation—were of little interest to a court besotted with sea otter pelts. Steller died in 1746 at the age of 37, convinced he had failed. But Steller's depictions of Alaska inspire new generations of naturalists, with their call not to plunder, but to protect and preserve.

LEFT: FAMED FOR ITS LARGE
POPULATION OF GRIZZLIES, THE
MCNEIL RIVER STATE GAME
PRESERVE DRAWS
PHOTOGRAPHERS FROM ALL
OVER THE WORLD.

ABOVE: GRIZZLY
(*URSUS HORRIBILIS*).

Other populations are found among the many indentations of Prince William Sound. A 15,000-square-mile maze of water, ice, and islands, the sound is dominated by oil and fishing. Valdez is its major port. Cradled between fjords and mountains, Valdez burst into being during the Klondike gold rush, but misfortune has occasionally slowed its course. Along with many other Alaskan towns, Valdez was gutted by the 1964 earthquake. Rebuilt afterward in a different place, Valdez regained economic health during the 1970s, when it became the terminus for the 800-mile-long trans-Alaska pipeline. But tragedy again befell the town in March of 1989 with the nation's worst oil spill. Ironically, efforts to repair the spill have created another prosperous period for Valdez.

A highway links Valdez to other Southcentral areas, but most Prince William Sound communities can only be reached by water or air. Whittier, in the western sound, is the center of small boat traffic and an Alaska Marine Highway System ferry port. Recreational activities in the area include hiking, sea kayaking, and scuba diving. Cordova, another major harbor, stands in serene isolation, almost totally supported by commercial fishing. Majestic Mount Eccles looms over this town of 2,000. East of Cordova, the Copper River drains into the Gulf of Alaska. Fishermen from around the world seek the river's salmon. The mudflats of the Copper River Delta lure lavish populations of migrating waterfowl and shorebirds. Species include the world's largest concentration of trumpeter swans and thousands of sandhill cranes.

Bordering the southwest arc of Prince William Sound is the Kenai Peninsula. Edged by rugged peaks on its eastern and southern boundaries, the peninsula rises between the Gulf of Alaska and Cook Inlet. Petroleum reserves were discovered here in the 1950s, and the oil industry remains important. But the area is also famous for its fishing, particularly along the 75-mile Kenai River. Much of the peninsula is contained in the Kenai National Wildlife Refuge, which consists of over 2 million acres. Special features of the refuge are glacial formations, moose habitat, and a king salmon fishery.

Alluring towns fleck the Kenai Peninsula, many of them bearing traces of early Russian occupation. Seldovia boasts an incomparable view: Kachemak Bay, Cook Inlet, and four active volcanoes. Artists frequent the pleasant enclave of Halibut Cove, formerly the site of herring salteries and fox farms. Gracefully settled upon a bluff and gazing into Mounts Iliamna and Redoubt is Old Ninilchik, where there once existed a Russian penal colony and a trapper's base. Another impressive setting belongs to Homer, a town of around 4,500. Pressed against the halibut-rich waters of Kachemak Bay, Homer spills along a 5-mile spit, the Alaska Range its dramatic northern backdrop. Boats depart from this small town to Peterson Bay, where pools brim with giant sunflower starfish, bright sea anemones, and moon snails. On nearby Gull Island, puffins, murres, and cormorants nest.

Throughout the Southcentral region, sharp peaks leap from the floors of broad river valleys and mountain groups crown the landscape. On Southcentral's eastern edge towers the Wrangell–St. Elias Range, offering some of Alaska's most heart-stopping scenery. Here snowcapped peaks ascend in compact huddles, many exceeding 16,000 feet. The Wrangell–St. Elias mountains catch storms formed in the Gulf of Alaska, resulting in awesome ice fields. On slopes and in river valleys here, flora and fauna flourish. Varied habitats hold Dall sheep, bears, caribou, and many types of birds. Along with Kluane National Park, its Canadian neighbor, and the Tetlin Wildlife Refuge, on Alaska's eastern border, the Wrangell–St. Elias National Park and Preserve was declared a United Nations World Heritage Site in 1984.

Measuring over 13 million acres, the preserve is the world's biggest parkland, and its treasures are many. The fan-shaped Malaspina Glacier covers an area the size of Rhode Island. From Chitistone and Nizina canyons a 400-foot waterfall cascades. Trails crisscross the lower elevations. Remains of Native villages, fur-trading posts, gold camps, and a copper mine imprint the human past. They are tiny strokes on a natural canvas that is inconceivably vast, immeasurably old.

TOP: A FISHING BOAT AT ANCHOR IN COOK INLET.

ABOVE: HALIBUT ARE PROLIFIC IN THE WATERS ALONG THE KENAI PENINSULA.

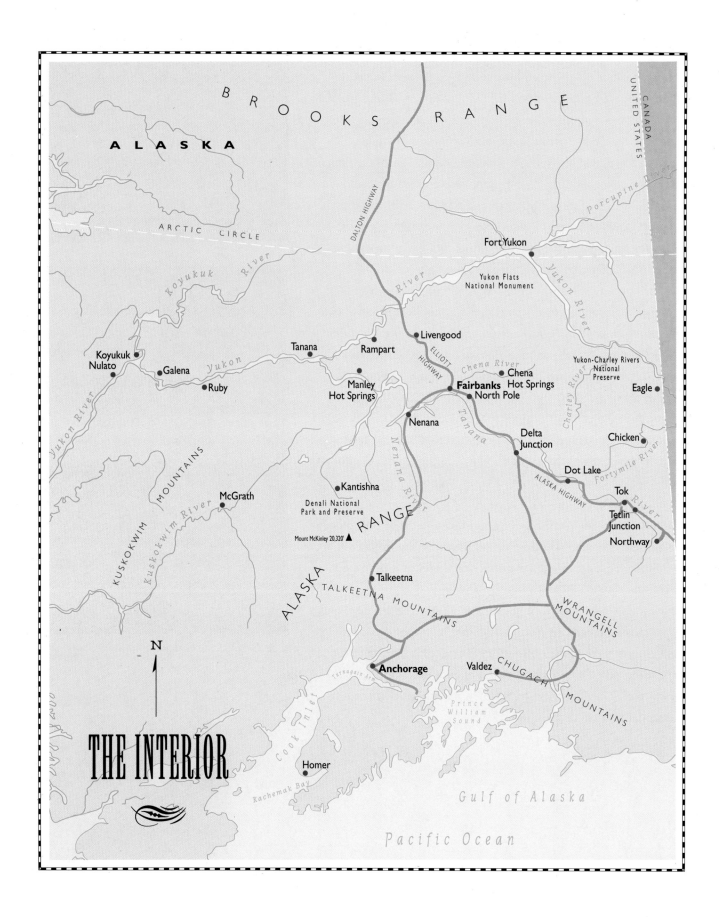

B R O O K S   R A N G E

ALASKA

ARCTIC   CIRCLE

DALTON HIGHWAY

Koyukuk River

Porcupine River

CANADA
UNITED STATES

Fort Yukon

Yukon Flats
National Monument

Yukon River

River

Livengood

Tanana
Rampart

ELLIOTT
HIGHWAY

Chena River

Chena
Hot Springs

Yukon-Charley Rivers
National
Preserve

Koyukuk
Nulato

Galena

Ruby

Yukon

Manley
Hot Springs

Fairbanks
North Pole

Charley River

Eagle

Yukon River

Nenana

Tanana

Delta
Junction

Chicken

Fortymile River

KUSKOKWIM   MOUNTAINS

Nenana River

Dot Lake

ALASKA HIGHWAY

Tok

River

Kantishna

McGrath

Kuskokwim River

Denali National
Park and Preserve

Mount McKinley 20,320' ▲

RANGE

Tetlin
Junction

Northway

ALASKA

TALKEETNA MOUNTAINS

WRANGELL
MOUNTAINS

200

Talkeetna

N

Anchorage

Turnagain Arm

Valdez

CHUGACH

MOUNTAINS

Prince
William
Sound

THE INTERIOR

Cook Inlet

Homer

Kachemak Bay

Gulf of Alaska

Pacific Ocean

The Heart of the Country

RIGHT: THE ATHAPASKANS OF
THE INTERIOR ARE FAMED FOR
THEIR ORNATE BEADWORK.

OVERLEAF: MAJESTIC MOUNT
MCKINLEY IS THE CONTINENT'S
HIGHEST MOUNTAIN AND THE
MOST POPULAR TOURIST
ATTRACTION IN ALASKA.

Moody alchemists, mountains create weather of their own. Their great height and massive shapes speak to the atmosphere in singular ways, sometimes with violent and unpredictable results. Nearby, skies may be clear. But lofty peaks can stand apart, cloaking themselves in clouds. They hurl rain and snow upon those who dare to ascend. Visitors to Talkeetna, a small town basking in its proximity to Mount McKinley, frequently wait to catch a glimpse of the mountain's elusive face. All of a sudden, the clouds pass. Bush pilots bustle to load passengers and cargo. Interior Alaska's greatest icon stands close enough to touch, its glaciers shimmering bright as jewelry.

At 20,320 feet, Mount McKinley is not only the highest peak in the Alaska Range, it is the tallest in North America, soaring over 3.5 miles from the valley floor. To the Tanaina Indians of the region, the mountain was simply *Denali*, or "The Great One." To the awestruck contemporary climber, it serves as a mecca, a potential conquest of irresistible allure.

Fearful of the effects of a human onslaught on the animal population and delicate terrain, authorities

established Mount McKinley National Park as a refuge in 1917, and it was recently renamed the Denali National Park and Preserve. While Mount McKinley is often aloof, the refuge's views of rare habitats and fragile ecosystems are easily approached. Located near the southern edge of the Interior region, the enormous park lies 120 miles south of Fairbanks and 240 miles north of Anchorage. The park protects a number of wildlife species. Grizzly bears, caribou, moose, and Dall sheep are among the many creatures living in the 6-million-acre preserve; birds include the great horned owl and willow ptarmigan, Alaska's state bird. Other distinctive natural features are Wonder Lake and Savage River Canyon. Paddlers enjoy the slow-moving waters of the Kantishna River. The river's route is an ancient one connecting the Tanana and Kuskokwim rivers, and it was later frequented by prospectors and trappers.

While many will journey to Denali by automobile, the more romantic choice is the Alaska Railroad. Constructed by the federal government in the first part of the century, the railroad was acquired by the state in the mid-1980s. Originating in the seaport of Seward, the 450-mile route passes broad lowlands, braided streams, and mountain vistas. Finished during the presidency of Warren Harding, the railroad may represent the only happy legacy of that troubled administration. Buoyed by the completion of the route in 1923, Harding gamely traveled all the way to the town of Nenana to drive the Golden Spike. Harding believed the promise of Alaska's resources was great, and his prescience would be borne out.

Harding was right not only about the existence of oil in the Territory but also about the importance of the railroad in Alaska's future. With the Interior's mighty rivers, the train opened up the heartland of Alaska, providing an avenue for the explorer, prospector, and settler. While only a handful of people occupied the Interior as recently as one century ago, the region's inhabitants now constitute around 20 percent of the state's population.

At 28,000 people, Fairbanks is by far the largest town in the Interior. Log cabins join sleek modern buildings in the city, which lies within the broad basin of the Tanana River valley. Founded in a fury by freewheeling gold seekers around the turn of the century, this community on the Chena River was catapulted from

THE DOGSLED HOUSE AT
DENALI NATIONAL PARK
AND PRESERVE.

OPPOSITE: THE ALASKA
RAILROAD OFFERS PANORAMAS
OF THE INTERIOR.

a muddy outpost to Alaska's wealthiest community. Fairbanks's fondness for those feisty ancestors is recalled in Alaskaland, a village of houses, shops, and mining equipment celebrating the city's history. During the summer, the *Discovery III* riverboat tours the Chena and Tanana rivers, gently transporting visitors back to the sternwheeler days.

Fairbanksans look to the future as well as the past. Based on a hillside outside of town, the University of Alaska draws scholars from all over the world. Courses range from the study of ancient Native cultures to space-age arctic technology. Scientists at the school's distinguished Geophysical Institute explore the North Country's unique physical characteristics, examining glaciology and the aurora borealis.

University programs also encourage agriculture in the state. As farmers discovered in the Matanuska Valley, Alaska's growing seasons are short but intensely productive. In the Tanana River valley, the major agricultural area of the Interior and potentially the state's richest farming region, robust harvests of potatoes, cabbage, and grains are common. Huge grain farms, some as large as 2,000 acres, sprawl across the landscape outside of Delta Junction.

Delta Junction is also the official end of the Alaska Highway, the 1,500-mile road starting in Dawson Creek, British Columbia, and linking Alaska to the Lower 48 states. Feverishly constructed during World War II, the highway quickly outgrew its role as a military route. Now it guides motorists through formerly impassable wilderness, introducing them to such colorful Interior communities as Dot Lake and Tok.

Loyalties run deep in the Interior, but the land can ask stern tribute. Cradled between the Brooks and Alaska ranges, the region has widely varying temperatures. Summers can be hot. Winter braces all that lives with legendary cold; temperatures routinely dip to 60 and 70 degrees below zero Fahrenheit. Extreme conditions shape unusual phenomena. Sometimes the air above the ground grows so chilled it cannot retain water vapor, and tiny ice crystals form. When the air also contains pollutants, the result is the arctic variation of smog.

Interior residents cope with the climate in typically spirited fashion. Winter carnivals take place throughout the region, in large and small settlements. Cold-weather sports such as

THE *DISCOVERY III*, A RESTORED PADDLEWHEELER, TRANSPORTS PEOPLE ALONG THE CHENA AND TANANA RIVERS OUTSIDE OF FAIRBANKS.

snowshoeing and sled dog racing are vigorously embraced. When the thermometer plummets, the soothing, steaming waters of Chena Hot Springs and Circle Hot Springs beckon, both located near Fairbanks.

Two different natural environments are found in the Interior. In the highlands and along the river valleys, white spruce, birch, and aspen predominate. Near the river lowlands, the mighty cottonwood grows. Black spruce sprouts in muskeg and bogs. The Russians called this boreal forest taiga, or "The Land of Little Sticks." Elsewhere in the region lies tundra, an almost treeless plain that hosts slow-growing vegetation such as grasses, sedges, and dwarf birch. Stunted by the cold and wind, these plants hug the earth. In the summer, hardy flowering plants accent the region with delicate colors and gentle scents.

Great rivers carve massive swaths through the Interior. At nearly 2,000 miles, the Yukon is the longest. Rising in Canada and emptying into the Bering Sea, the Yukon is the mother of all of the region's rivers. Even its tributaries are imposing. The Porcupine, Koyukuk, and Tanana all exceed 500 miles. In the winter, ice stills much of the Yukon. But each spring, forceful currents break free in a mighty crush. Again the river becomes an artery, transporting food and goods to remote places.

For thousands of years, the Athapaskan Indians were people of the rivers. Often traveling great distances, they followed the caribou and moose. From the rivers they took fish, especially salmon, which they preserved by drying and smoking. Athapaskans are famed for their hunting and fishing prowess, and for painstaking artwork. Intricate floral beadwork on clothing and other items is sought by collectors and museums around the world.

Athapaskan villages continue to flourish along the Yukon. Galena thrives as a tourist center and transportation hub. The town is located at the edge of the Koyukuk National Wildlife Refuge, site of an active dune field. (Its immense drifts shaped over eons by windblown deposits, the field is one of only two in northern Alaska.) Commercial fishing helps sustain beautiful Rampart, where gold mines still operate. Ruby is the site of a historic roadhouse. Residents in these and other Interior communities bridge two centuries: many follow traditional subsistence lifestyles, but are also employed in modern

THE WOLF RANGES THROUGHOUT MUCH OF ALASKA, USUALLY TRAVELING IN PACKS.

MOUNT MCKINLEY IS
ESPECIALLY FAVORED BY HIKERS
AND SKIERS, WHO PRIZE ITS
MANY CHALLENGING TRAILS.

professions—teaching, firefighting, and government work.

European settlement in the Interior began in the early to middle 1800s, but its pace was more leisurely than that of surrounding regions. The Russians established a fur-trading post at Nulato in 1838, and the British followed with one at Fort Yukon, 8 miles north of the Arctic Circle, in 1847. Surveyors would lead the next push through the countryside, and the Western Union Telegraph Expedition briefly attempted to set lines. While the project was later abandoned, it focused new attention on the Interior. In the course of their explorations, naturalists like William Dall wrote about the richness of the region, and the diverse species living within it. With each publication came another wave of development, as trapper, miner, missionary, and settler ventured out.

After gold was discovered in Fortymile River in the 1880s, fortune seekers flocked north. Soon stampeders overwhelmed tiny communities such as Circle, located near the Yukon Territory border. Pressed between mountain bluffs and river flats, the settlement is a popular launching spot for Yukon River boaters.

Another departure point for Yukon River floaters is Eagle. Once a boat landing, the town has carefully restored a number of stately buildings. Eagle is also the headquarters of the 2.5-million-acre Yukon-Charley Rivers National Preserve. More than 200 species of birds are drawn to the preserve, which lies along a major flyway for waterfowl. Rocky peaks contain habitat for the peregrine falcon. The rivers host many fish, including king, coho, and chum salmon. Unlike the much-visited Yukon, the Charley River watershed is virtually untouched. Access to the headwaters of the river for float trips is primarily by helicopter.

The broad Yukon flows slowly through the park, passing old mining camps, where long-abandoned cabins line the river's edge. Relics and artifacts recall the sagas of those indomitable early settlers, how tenaciously they clung to the dream of gold.

NORTHERN LIGHTS

Most northern cultures invented legends about the aurora borealis, among nature's most mesmerizing events. Eskimos believed these swirling apparitions were the spirits of the dead, and that by whistling they could summon them near. Explorers' diaries are filled with accounts of their color illuminating the sky in complex displays.

The northern lights have for many years intrigued the scientist and the philosopher. Because auroral storms can severely disrupt modern communications, experts continue to search for clues about their causes. A center for such study is the Geophysical Institute at the University of Alaska in Fairbanks.

For many years it was understood that the lights were an electrical phenomenon, magnetic disturbances caused by the sun colliding with atoms in the upper air. But the invention of specialized cameras and jet airplanes revealed much more about the aurora. One discovery is that the lights have a global mirror image; they appear at the same time in the southern hemisphere, where they're known as the aurora australis.

Another finding is that the aurora can be seen more frequently in some places than in others. South of the magnetic north pole, the aurora may flash 200 times a year. But in central Mexico, it is visible only a few nights each decade.

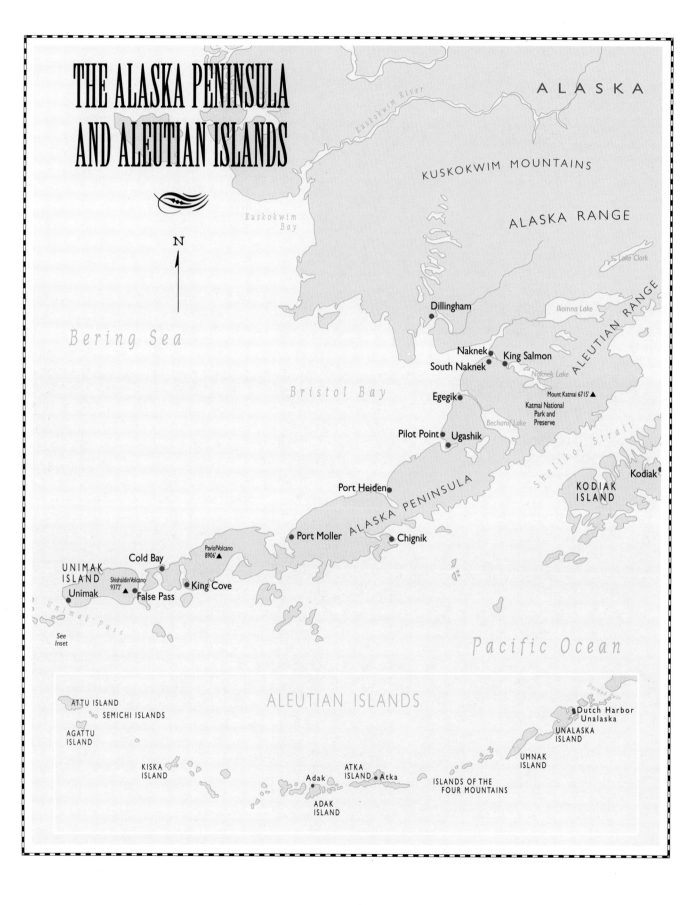

THE ALASKA PENINSULA AND ALEUTIAN ISLANDS

N

ALASKA

Kuskokwim River

KUSKOKWIM MOUNTAINS

ALASKA RANGE

S Lake Clark

Kuskokwim Bay

Iliamna Lake

Bering Sea

Dillingham

ALEUTIAN RANGE

Naknek
King Salmon
South Naknek

Naknek Lake

Bristol Bay

Egegik

Mount Katmai 6715' ▲

Katmai National
Park and
Preserve

Becharof Lake

Pilot Point
Ugashik

Shelikof Strait

KODIAK
ISLAND

Kodiak

Port Heiden

ALASKA PENINSULA

Port Moller
Chignik

Cold Bay

Pavlof Volcano
8906' ▲

UNIMAK
ISLAND

Shishaldin Volcano
9372' ▲

Unimak
False Pass

King Cove

Unimak Pass

See
Inset

Pacific Ocean

ALEUTIAN ISLANDS

Unimak Pass

ATTU ISLAND
SEMICHI ISLANDS

Dutch Harbor
Unalaska

AGATTU
ISLAND

UNALASKA
ISLAND

KISKA
ISLAND

UMNAK
ISLAND

Adak

ATKA
ISLAND Atka

ISLANDS OF THE
FOUR MOUNTAINS

ADAK
ISLAND

The Land of Smoky Seas

Nature bore southwestern Alaska in a series of fiery storms. Convulsions deep beneath the seabed thrust volcanoes to the surface, leaving a chain of islands arcing gently out from a rocky peninsula. This thin spine separates two volatile bodies of water, the Pacific Ocean and the Bering Sea. Around the 1,200-mile chain that makes up the Aleutian Islands, cold arctic waters collide with the warm Japanese Current, forcing weather of fearsome power. To the Aleuts, the Natives who have lived here for thousands of years, it is the Land of Smoky Seas.

Consisting of hundreds of islands, most of them uninhabited, the Aleutian Chain is the northern link in what scientists refer to as the Ring of Fire. Considered the world's most unstable region because of frequent eruptions and earthquakes, the ring extends along the Pacific Rim from Alaska to South America. Scores of volcanoes punctuate this fiery terrain. In Alaska, the ring is dominated by the rugged Aleutian Range.

Only a handful of people live in this vast region consisting of the Aleutian and Pribilof islands and the Alaska Peninsula. Commercial fishing and government employment support most of the area's residents, who share an affection for its stark, wild spaces.

RIGHT: A VOLCANO ON ONE OF THE ISLANDS OF THE FOUR MOUNTAINS, AN ALEUTIAN GROUP.

Threaded by lakes and rivers, the Alaska Peninsula is bordered on one side by the Pacific. At its base lies Katmai National Park and Preserve, established to protect the environs of one of history's most violent volcanic eruptions. Called the Valley of Ten Thousand Smokes, the 40-square-mile spot is still covered with a deep layer of ash several hundred feet deep from the eruption of Novarupta Volcano in 1912. While plumes of steam no longer curl from the ground, the landscape remains eerie, as if the explosion took place days before. But most of the preserve's 4 million acres of forests and fjords can be characterized by plenty rather than destruction. Wildlife is prolific, and many species attain large size, especially the coastal grizzlies. Among the two-dozen types of fish found in the lakes and rivers of the park are 20-pound rainbow trout.

The Alaska Peninsula National Wildlife Refuge provides habitat for millions of waterfowl; the world's entire population of emperor geese migrates here each spring. Cold Bay, the transportation center for the region, is among the places providing airplane access to the park. This town of 300 is also the gateway for the Izembek National Wildlife Refuge, one of the state's oldest. Eelgrass beds float in the park's lagoons, luring the colorful Steller eider and black brant. Shorebirds flock in limitless numbers, sometimes resembling an enormous dark cloth rippling across the sky.

The Aleutians are the world's longest archipelago. Windswept and fog-enshrouded much of the time, the small islands are densely blanketed in shrubs, herbaceous plants, grasses, and moss. With the tiny Pribilofs, their neighbors to the north, they can experience summers of intensity. Bright wildflowers bloom, and tundra along exposed ridges makes a dense green carpet. Island temperatures are moderate, ranging from 30 to 50 degrees Fahrenheit throughout the year.

Much of the area is encompassed by a single park, the Alaska Maritime Wildlife Refuge. Including nearly all of the Aleutians and the Pribilofs, the refuge exceeds 35 million acres, stretching from Port Franklin on the Chukchi Sea to southeastern Alaska. Rimmed by treacherous shorelines, the park is home to huge populations of marine birds and thousands of sea mammals.

Webs of kelp and algae fill the waters surrounding the Aleutians with nutrients, ensuring the presence of whales, sea

OPPOSITE: WILLOWS SPROUT BELOW VOLCANIC ASH WALLS IN THE RIVER LETHE GORGE, VALLEY OF TEN THOUSAND SMOKES, KATMAI NATIONAL PARK AND PRESERVE.

ABOVE: TUFTED PUFFINS ON THE ALASKA PENINSULA.

NAKNEK LAKE, ONE OF THE
MANY CRYSTALLINE WILDERNESS
LAKES IN KATMAI NATIONAL
PARK AND PRESERVE.

lions, porpoises, fur seals, harbor seals, and sea otters. These animals have long fed the Natives, and helped to shape their culture. The Aleuts captured the animals in one-man *baidarkas*, extremely efficient skin-covered kayaks. Each man owned at least one single-hatch *baidarka*, and a community's strength was measured in the number of vessels it could muster.

Aleut villages were usually perched above the water's edge, rarely inland, providing better access to the resources of the sea. Before the Europeans' arrival, there were many such settlements scattered across the Aleutian Chain. From the islands' interiors the Aleuts gathered berries, greens, and roots. Ancient homes were large communal structures of sod and logs built partially underground. Later the Aleuts lived in smaller enclosures, or *barabaras*. Whalebones might support the dwellings, and translucent sealskin served as windows.

Close relatives of the Eskimo, whose language is similar, Aleuts numbered perhaps 25,000 when the Russian *promyshlenniki*, or fur traders, arrived. Emboldened by explorers' ecstatic accounts in the mid-1700s, the traders stormed the islands for several decades. The Natives' superior hunting skills were tapped, as the Russians conscripted them to gather sea otter pelts as far south as California.

One animal the Russians hunted no longer exists. Georg Steller, the German naturalist who accompanied the Bering expedition, described the unusual sea cow, a species that was once numerous. Twenty-five feet long, the cow had the appearance of an enormous seal with a fishlike tail. Just one-quarter century after its discovery by the Europeans, who sought it for food, the sea cow was extinct.

The Russians abandoned Alaska when its fur-trading operations diminished, but many reminders of this period linger in southwest Alaska. Russian architecture still decorates the streets of Kodiak, one of Alaska's most breathtaking communities. On Kodiak Island, misty fjords hem the coastline and sharp summits climb as high as 4,000 feet above sea level. Known as the Emerald Island, Kodiak shimmers during vibrant summers with tall green grass and meadows of flowers.

Elegant Russian Orthodox churches—many painted in rich pastels of pink and yellow—continue to enliven villages on the Pribilofs and on the Aleutians, where they remain centers of community life. While the Russians altered traditional forms of worship, priests also conveyed a tool of cultural preservation by assisting in the creation of an Aleut alphabet.

With the advent of World War II, the Aleutians again captured the world's attention. Suddenly the islands assumed strategic significance. In June of 1942, the Japanese invaded Attu and Kiska islands. The United States responded with a buildup of harbors, airports, and bases. By 1943, the Japanese withdrew. Fifty years later, U.S. military installations remain. The Navy supports a base of 5,000 on Adak Island, the Air Force a much smaller installation on Shemya.

Nourished by a strong fishing industry, the Aleut economy continues to grow. Commerce is concentrated in Unalaska and Dutch Harbor, two cities united by a bridge on the northern side of Unalaska Island. Unalaska derives from the Aleut word *agunalaksh*, meaning "the shores where the sea breaks its back." Legendary winds have not hampered the town's development. Today it is among the country's most productive seafood

A Soviet stern trawler off the Bering Sea Coast at the 200-mile limit.

OPPOSITE: Workers process fish in one of Kodiak's many commercial plants.

processing ports, with many canneries. An early headquarters for the Russian-American Company, Unalaska was also a major stop for ships heading to and from the Nome gold fields.

The prosperous village of Sand Point also originated as a supply center. Located on the Shumagin Islands, this community of 900 boasts a locally owned crab and salmon fishing fleet.

Fishing also bolsters the economy of the Pribilofs, where fur seal harvesting has long dominated activity. Creating a deafening chorus, one million northern fur seals still gather on the remote shores of St. Paul and St. George islands each summer, and their management is overseen by the Aleut residents. Tourism is also increasing in these austerely beautiful outposts. In the larger community of St. Paul, gift shops sell carved ivory pieces and fur seal garments. On Black Diamond Hill, visitors uncover shiny crystals of augite, some of gem size.

With economic development has come political participation. A profusion of Native organizations has unified many voices. The groups increasingly play prominent parts in state and federal planning, enlarging the Aleuts' role in the state's future development.

Efforts are also under way to restore the land of the Aleutians to full health. On some uninhabited, grassy islands, cattle are being rounded up to protect eroded soil. On others, traps catch foxes loose from abandoned fur-farming ventures, permitting seabirds to nest in peace. Isolated islands have become magnets for birders from around the world. There will never be another family of sea cows swimming peacefully in the offshore kelp beds. But sea otters are once again great in number, and can be seen playing in the harbors and searching for shellfish. Puffins dive from their sea-cliff ledges. Falcons and hawks hunt the skies. Bald eagles glide over beaches, where the surf rolls shoreward in an endless procession of waves.

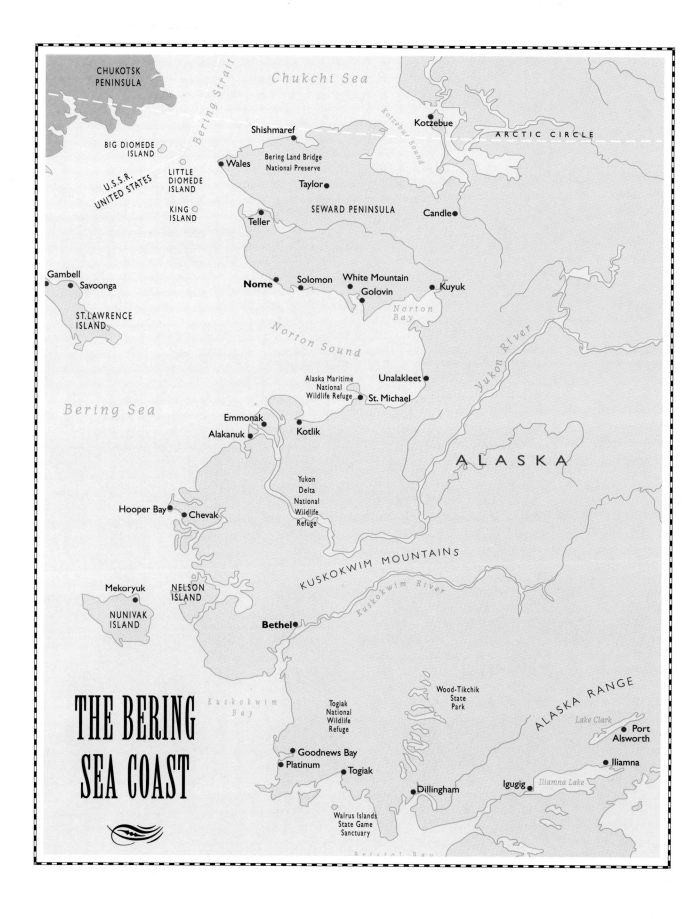

CHUKOTSK
PENINSULA

Chukchi Sea

Bering Strait

Shishmaref

Kotzebue

Kotzebue Sound

ARCTIC CIRCLE

BIG DIOMEDE
ISLAND

Wales

Bering Land Bridge
National Preserve

U.S.S.R.
UNITED STATES

LITTLE
DIOMEDE
ISLAND

Taylor

SEWARD PENINSULA

Candle

KING
ISLAND

Teller

Gambell
Savoonga

Nome   Solomon   White Mountain
Golovin   Kuyuk

ST. LAWRENCE
ISLAND

*Norton
Bay*

Norton Sound

Yukon River

Bering Sea

Unalakleet

Alaska Maritime
National
Wildlife Refuge

St. Michael

Emmonak
Alakanuk   Kotlik

ALASKA

Yukon
Delta
National
Wildlife
Refuge

Hooper Bay   Chevak

KUSKOKWIM MOUNTAINS

Kuskokwim River

Mekoryuk   NELSON
ISLAND

NUNIVAK
ISLAND

Bethel

Wood-Tikchik
State
Park

ALASKA RANGE

Lake Clark

Port
Alsworth

THE BERING
SEA COAST

*Kuskokwim
Bay*

Togiak
National
Wildlife
Refuge

Goodnews Bay
Platinum   Togiak

Dillingham

Igugig

Iliamna

Iliamna Lake

Walrus Islands
State Game
Sanctuary

Bristol Bay

The Bridge to Long Ago

Beach grass billows from clotheslines along the Bering Sea Coast, and gut parkas balloon in the brisk wind. For generations, the region's indigenous peoples have created items of beauty and utility from nature's simplest products. Dried and braided, the grass is woven into elaborate baskets. Trimmed with dyed tufts of hair from seals or other animals, the parkas will protect their wearers from the spring rains. Such time-honored transformations take place amid many symbols of modern life. From beneath the earth, gold, platinum, tin, and mercury enrich an economy long ruled by hunting and fishing.

The Bering Sea Coast area extends from the head of Bristol Bay to the north shore of the Seward Peninsula, near the Arctic Circle. Within the region are Bering Sea islands, among them St. Lawrence and Nunivak. The Inupiat and Yupik Eskimos and the Athapaskan Indians are the primary residents. Natural jewels include rugged mountains, fishing bays of extraordinary richness, and a massive river delta. Its movement accelerated by broad expanses of flatland, the wind is a steady presence. Seasons are distinct. Summer paints the tiny growths characteristic of tundra vegetation. The fall's crisp temperatures color

RIGHT: IVORY HAS LONG BEEN A POPULAR MEDIUM AMONG NATIVE ARTISANS IN THE BERING SEA COAST REGION.

DISCOVER ALASKA

low-growing cranberry plants, splashing whole slopes a brilliant red. Winters can be severe, especially in the northern reaches. But to the south, the sea moderates the cold, often restraining it to between zero and 30 degrees Fahrenheit. Precipitation also varies, falling more heavily inland.

So plenteous are the attributes of the mammoth Bering Sea Coast area that it cannot easily be spoken of as one region. More frequently it is divided into three: the Seward Peninsula, the Yukon-Kuskokwim Delta, and Bristol Bay.

The Seward Peninsula is the northernmost section of the Bering Sea Coast. Extending 200 miles into the icy waters, its border reaches to within a few miles of the Soviet Union. From earliest times, the area has straddled two worlds. Little Diomede Island, off the tip of the peninsula, once served as a crossroads between Siberia and the Alaska mainland. Early Yupik Eskimos from the village of Inalik, now called Diomede, traded freely between the two continents, sharing furs and establishing alliances. But contact between Diomede and Big Diomede Island, a Soviet territory, was shattered following World War II. As feelings thaw between East and West, communities long separated may meet once again.

The 2.8-million-acre Bering Land Bridge National Preserve marks another passage, commemorating one of history's most significant migrations. The preserve lies just below the Arctic Circle on the Seward Peninsula. Scientists believe that, perhaps 25,000 years ago, the area was part of a 900-mile-wide bridge linking Asia and North America. Formed by swelling glaciers and depleted seas, the path opened a route to the New World for people, animals, and plants. Evidence of some of these old journeys dates back 10,000 years. Souvenirs left by the ancient travelers include ivory and bone carvings and stone cairns. Signs of nature's complex patterns also endure. Low-rimmed volcanoes, lava flows, and hot springs draw visitors to the preserve.

Vestiges of the past also dominate St. Lawrence, a harshly beautiful island some 200 miles off the mainland. St. Lawrence has two major settlements, Gambell and Savoonga, and a number of archaeological sites. Predominantly a whaling community, the island is also celebrated for its precious fossil ivory. Often embedded within historical areas or along beaches, the ivory is a favored material for many local artists.

OPPOSITE: AN ESKIMO WOMAN FROM KIANA CLEANS SALMON WITH AN *ULU*, OR TRADITIONAL CURVED KNIFE.

BELOW: MUCH THE WAY THEIR ANCESTORS DID, THESE ESKIMOS BEGIN A HUNT NEAR BIG DIOMEDE ISLAND.

Nome is the largest community in northwest Alaska, and marks the end of the Iditarod Trail Sled Dog Race. Hundreds withstand the March cold to await victors in the contest, a grueling trek from Anchorage. But celebrity is not novel in this town of 4,000. Gold gave the hardy city its start in 1898. Then, 20,000 frenzied stampeders swarmed its muddy streets; campsites stretched into infinity along its "golden beaches." Gold is still extracted by dredging in the area, but contemporary Nome is financially diversified. The starting point for trips to arctic villages such as Shishmaref and Teller, Nome hosts numerous annual events, including the Bering Sea Ice Golf Classic.

No longer inhabited, the village of Ukivok on King Island remains a powerful invocation of the spirit of the Seward Peninsula. Few sites are so dramatic as this one, where abandoned wood-frame dwellings cling precariously to a King Island hillside. Inupiat Eskimos dwelled on this island, a rocky pinnacle jutting 1,100 feet above the Bering Sea. In the 1950s, people relocated. But the island was not forgotten. Former residents created the King Island Inupiat Singers and Dancers, resurrecting legends that had sustained their people for centuries. Some villagers still return to the island each summer to harvest wild bird eggs, gather greens, and hunt walrus in the tradition of their ancestors.

TOP: SLED DOG RACING IS A PASSION THROUGHOUT ALASKA.

ABOVE: THE ONLY PARKING METER IN NOME, THE UNOFFICIAL CAPITAL OF NORTHWESTERN ALASKA.

The coastal cliffs and glacial valleys of the Ahklun Mountains separate Bristol Bay from one of the world's great river deltas, the Yukon-Kuskokwim. A million streams, sloughs, ponds, and lakes cross the land like a lattice, supporting colonies of plant and animal life. The delta is a summer nesting ground for millions of ducks, geese, and swans, including 80 percent of the world's emperor and Canada geese.

Almost all of the delta is encompassed in the Yukon Delta National Wildlife Refuge, a 19-million-acre park. Caribou, grizzlies, and wolves roam the northern hills. The park also includes Nunivak Island, where rolling tundra and precipitous sea cliffs are home to herds of musk-oxen and reindeer.

Over 50 Yupik Eskimo villages huddle about the Kuskokwim and Yukon river basins. Bethel, located at the head of Kuskokwim Bay and possessing a population of 5,000, is by far the largest, and the area's financial and political heart. A new visitor center and museum offer exhibits of traditional Native tools and clothing.

DISCOVER ALASKA

Along the streets of Bethel, the Yupik dialect continues to be widely spoken. Commercial fishing is the base of Bethel's economy, but here, as elsewhere on the coast, old pursuits are still practiced.

Animals have never been plentiful in the treeless river delta. Whatever the Yupik caught was apportioned with reverence, a sign of a deeply held code. The Yupik believed a dead animal would return, offering itself to another generation. If respectfully taken, the animal would again feed their children and their children's children.

Remote rivers like the Togiak and Tikchik empty into Bristol Bay, a fishing area of extraordinary abundance. Each summer, millions of salmon enter the river drainages on the way to spawning grounds. King salmon come first, followed by red and chum, pink, and finally silver. Armed with gill nets, fishermen brave the choppy waters of the bay. Many crowd the harbor of Dillingham, a town of 2,100 and the area's commercial capital.

Communities surrounding the bay, such as Iliamna, Mankjoitak, and Levelock, are dominated by canneries. Villages share memories of the Russian period, which survives in the Russian Orthodox churches of Ekuk, Iguigig, and Kokhanok. One settlement, Port Alsworth, is among Alaska's most exquisite. Situated on tranquil Lake Clark, a spawning grounds for the Bristol Bay red salmon run, Port Alsworth holds Tanalian Falls and the ruins of historic Kijik village. The town is the headquarters for Lake Clark National Park and Preserve, featuring mountain valleys and blue-green glaciers.

Birds migrate to Bristol Bay from around the world. At the Togiak National Wildlife Refuge west of Dillingham, there are emperor geese, Steller eiders, harlequin ducks, and black scoters. Walrus Islands State Game Sanctuary is a prime viewing spot for the bull walrus. As the ice recedes, between 5,000 and 10,000 of the male mammals return each spring, temporarily leaving the females and young behind at their feeding grounds. In the wake of the walrus follow hundreds of thousands of seabirds.

The 1.5-million-acre Wood-Tikchik State Park also adjoins Bristol Bay. The largest state park in the United States, the Wood-Tikchik is shadowed by mountains some 3,000 to 5,000 feet in height. Countless crystalline lakes, high alpine valleys, and numerous islands form a landscape of bright splendor.

AFTER THEY WERE DECIMATED BY OVERHUNTING, MUSK-OXEN WERE REINTRODUCED TO ALASKA A CENTURY AGO. TODAY THEIR UNDERHAIR IS WOVEN INTO *QIVIUT*, A YARN OF UNSURPASSED SOFTNESS.

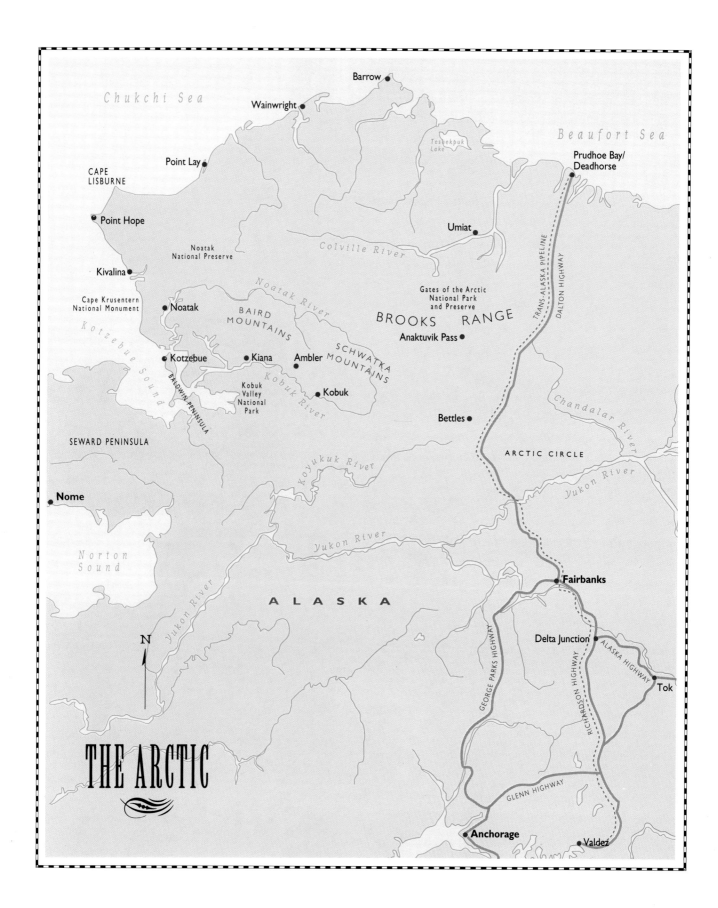

A Timeless World of White

The great sea
Has sent me adrift.
It moves me
As the weed in a great
river.
Earth and the great
weather,
Move me,
Have carried me away
And move my inward
parts with joy.

—Eskimo poem

The world of the Eskimo is cold and white and bountiful. For millennia, the Inupiat Eskimos ingeniously adapted to the exacting conditions of Alaska's Arctic, the region that sits across the top of the state like a crown of ice. From the oceans, they hunted seals, sea lions, walruses, and whales. Inland, they followed the caribou. These master craftsmen impressed utility and beauty on every part of a captured animal. Tusks of walrus became tools, and skin was stretched into *umiaks*, their large, flat-bottomed boats. Rain suits were fashioned from the intestines of seals. Accomplished tailors, the women transformed furs into elegant clothing of complex patterns.

To the Eskimo, the land could not be divided from the spirit. Dances and masks celebrated the connections existing between all things, the hunter and hunted. When a seal was slaughtered, its mouth was filled with water. In that way, if the animal's soul were thirsty, it would not be angry with the killer. Even today, there is communion between Eskimo and prey. Outside Point Hope, the oldest continuously inhabited settlement in North America, whalebones stand like pillars of a church. The bones mark gravesites within the stark arctic landscape.

RIGHT: THE GREAT MONARCH OF THE ARCTIC, THE POLAR BEAR MAY RANGE HUNDREDS OF MILES SEARCHING FOR FOOD.

The Alaskan Arctic spreads west along the crest of the Brooks Range to the headwaters of the Noatak River. From there, the boundary dips south past the community of Kobuk to the Arctic Circle and on to the Chukchi Sea. Like sentinels, snowy peaks guard the region, and gentle foothills ease toward the plain. An interlace of rivers and thousands of small lakes break the flat expanse. Pingo—wedges of ice surging from the permafrost—adds relief to the broad landscape.

Precipitation is scant in the Arctic and the winds are harsh. The Inupiat sought shelter in sod homes burrowed in the earth. Several families might share a single dwelling, its frame crafted from driftwood or whalebone. The Eskimos moved to campsites in the summer, reestablishing old alliances. When the Polish explorer Otto von Kotzebue arrived in 1816, he marveled not at the peoples' isolation but at the breadth of their reach. The Eskimos didn't covet the goods and arms he brought. They already possessed an exotic array of objects obtained through trade with distant Siberian relatives.

The romance of the Arctic is not new. The ancient Greeks told stories about a mysterious northern land, which they called Arktikos after the constellation Arktos, the Great Bear. In eighteenth- and nineteenth-century Europe, curiosity intensified into longing. Adventurers from many nations sought the Northwest Passage. Journeys were well publicized and ill conceived. Public fascination fanned the expeditions, making heroes of their leaders. But the Arctic's deep secrets were uncovered at a terrible price. Thousands perished, their ships ensnared by ice.

Not all arctic treasure was dangerous to reach. Decades ago, Eskimos knew of the presence of oil; it seeped about them on the coastal plain. But the resource interested few until 1968, when an immense field was discovered east of Barrow on the Beaufort Sea. The northern terminus of the trans-Alaska pipeline, Prudhoe Bay stands in strange contradiction. While arctic loons congregate in a nearby waterway, prefabricated structures house thousands of workers, giving the appearance of a colony on the moon. Drilling rigs roar on manmade islands. From deep in the earth, pumps work ceaselessly, sending millions of gallons of oil south to Valdez. Like a latter-day gold strike, the pipeline sparked an overnight bonanza of jobs and modern facilities. Faced with

OPPOSITE: AFTER ITS DISCOVERY ON THE NORTH SLOPE IN 1968, OIL QUICKLY BECAME ALASKA'S DOMINANT INDUSTRY. RIGS LIKE THIS ONE AT PRUDHOE BAY WORK 24 HOURS A DAY.

ABOVE: AN INUPIAT ESKIMO WOMAN FROM THE KOTZEBUE BASIN.

overwhelming change, Natives work to keep traditions alive.

Oil is the economic mainstay of much the Arctic, and Barrow is its commercial and political heart. The northernmost community in North America, Barrow is the seat of the North Slope Borough. Covering 88,000 square acres, the borough is the world's largest municipal government. Once an Eskimo village, Barrow rose to prominence during the era of whaling, when merchants and mariners crowded the streets. The mammal is still cherished in this community of 3,000. Strips of whale meat hang outside local Native homes, drying in the fierce wind. In April and May, whaling camps revive, as Native hunters return to an age-old pursuit. Residents search the sea for signs of the bowhead and beluga, rejoicing at a successful season.

Tourism, trapping, and fishing support Kotzebue, the hub of the southwestern Arctic. Centuries before the Europeans came, traders gathered here on the tip of the Baldwin Peninsula. Proximity to rivers and big game such as the polar bear enticed early inhabitants. Contemporary Kotzebue continues to be a meeting place. A dynamic waterfront and a sophisticated museum attract numerous visitors. During the annual Arctic Trades Fair, artisans journey here from distant points, displaying jade jewelry, delicate carvings, and whalebone masks.

Native artwork is also in evidence in Ambler, located near the confluence of the Ambler and Kobuk rivers. Forests of spruce and birch frame this tranquil community in the southwestern Arctic, where Native women fashion birchbark baskets and beaver hats. North of the town, the Jade Mountains stand, their peaks tinged in greenish-gray. Chunks of the gem are secreted amid its rocky slopes, some of great size. Outside the villages of Kobuk and Shungnak, old fishing trails line the Kobuk River. For generations, these ancient passageways have furnished a route to the caribou and to the sheefish teeming in nearby waters.

Spread along a sliver of land pointing into the Chukchi Sea, Point Hope may be the Arctic's most fertile historical landmark. Artifacts and the remains of dwellings establish the community's remarkable longevity; Point Hope is believed to be at least 2,500 years old. In the past, the waters off its coast were thick with marine mammals and the village was home to a large population. Today, the number of residents has dwindled to 600, and motorized vessels have supplanted dog teams as a means of

A CESSNA 185 FLOATPLANE TRAVELS OVER THE GATES OF THE ARCTIC NATIONAL PARK AND PRESERVE.

transportation. But Point Hope continues to venerate the old ways. Many men participate in the spring whale hunt, using skin boats similar to those of their ancestors. *Muktuk*, a delicacy made from the whale's outer skin layers, is still a popular dish.

Alaska's Arctic holds a wealth of parks, preserves, refuges, and monuments, each intended to protect wildlife populations and natural landscapes. Perhaps the best known is the Arctic National Wildlife Refuge. The refuge covers the northeast corner of the state and consists of over 19 million acres. While created to guard the migration routes of the Porcupine caribou herd, the park shelters many animals, ranging from hoary marmots to peregrine falcons to polar bears. The park's delicate vegetation and massive land forms face the threat of a competing interest: the refuge is a major oil prospect.

The centerpiece of the Gates of the Arctic National Park and Preserve is the Brooks Range. The range extends 600 miles from the Canadian border on the east to the Arctic Ocean on the west. Among its most dramatic features are the sharp granitic towers of the Arrigetch Peaks, whose name comes from an Eskimo word meaning "fingers of the hand outstretched." Six wild and scenic rivers flow through the Gates of the Arctic, one of the world's great wilderness areas. On the north slope of the Brooks Range lies Anaktuvuk Pass, home of the last remaining band of Nunamiut Eskimos. This group traditionally followed game, but settled permanently along this historic caribou route in the 1950s.

Unparalleled opportunities for river floating and kayaking are offered in the Kobuk Valley National Park, located in the middle portion of the Kobuk River. Within an easy walk of the river are the Great Kobuk Sand Dunes, wind-carved structures looming more than 100 feet tall.

Northwest of Kotzebue, Cape Krusenstern National Monument enshrines a rich chronicle of Arctic history. More than 100 beach ridges peek from this low moorland, documenting the record of thousands of years of human occupation. The interplay of sea and ice shaped the ridges, mostly used by Natives for hunting camps.

Today, along the outermost beach, Eskimos still hunt for seals, while at the shoreline, women wait to trim the catch.

THIS ALASKAN LODGE IS LOCATED IN THE ARCTIC COMMUNITY OF BETTLES, ON THE BANKS OF THE UPPER KOYUKUK RIVER.

Recommended Reading

Aigner, Jean, Robert Thorson, and eds. *Interior Alaska: A Journey Through Time*. Anchorage: The Alaska Geographic Society, 1986.

Bruder, Gerry. *Heroes of the Horizon: Flying Adventures of Alaska's Legendary Bush Pilots*. Bothell, Wash: Alaska Northwest Books™, 1991.

Christy, Jim. *Rough Road to the North: Travels Along the Alaska Highway*. New York: Doubleday, 1980.

Crandall, Alissa (photography), and Gloria J. Maschmeyer (text). *Along the Alaska Highway*. Bothell, Wash: Alaska Northwest Books™, 1991.

Dufresne, Frank. *No Room for Bears: A Wilderness Writer's Experiences with a Threatened Breed*. Bothell, Wash: Alaska Northwest Books™, 1991.

Dyson, George. *Baidarka: The Kayak*. Bothell, Wash: Alaska Northwest Books™, 1986.

Ford, Corey. *Where the Sea Breaks Its Back*. Boston: Little, Brown, 1966.

Haines, John. *The Stars, The Smoke, The Fire: 25 Years in the Northern Wilderness, a Memoir*. St. Paul: Graywolf Press, 1989.

Hulley, Clarence Charles. *Alaska: Past and Present* (3d ed.). Portland, Ore.: Binford and Morts, 1970.

Morgan, Lael. *And the Land Provides: Alaskan Natives in a Year of Transition*. Garden City, N.Y.: Anchor Press/Doubleday, 1974.

Muir, John. *Travels in Alaska*. Boston: Houghton Mifflin Company, 1879.

Nelson, Richard. *A Shadow of the Hunter: Stories of Eskimo Life*. Chicago.: University of Chicago Press, 1987.

Ray, Dorothy Jean. *Eskimo Masks: Art and Ceremony*. Seattle: University of Washington Press, 1967.

Schultz, Jeff (photography), and Bill Sherwonit (text). *Iditarod: The Great Race to Nome*. Bothell, Wash: Alaska Northwest Books™, 1991.

Sherwonit, Bill. *To the Top of Denali: Climbing Adventures on North America's Highest Peak*. Bothell, Wash: Alaska Northwest Books™, 1990.

Weeden, Robert. *Alaska: Promises to Keep*. Boston: Houghton Mifflin Company, 1978.

Index

Note: Italic numbers indicate photo captions. Frequently, that subject is also discussed in text on the same page.

Adak Island, U.S. Navy base on, 45
Admiralty Island, 16
agriculture, 24, 36
Ahklun Mountains, 52
Air Force (U.S.) bases, 22
air taxi services, 23
Alaska Highway, 36
Alaska Marine Highway System, 14, 28
Alaska Maritime Wildlife Refuge, 43
Alaska Peninsula National Wildlife Refuge, 43
Alaska Peninsula/Aleutian Islands: 40-47; climate, 41, 43; flora/fauna, 43, 46. *See also* Aleutian Islands
Alaska Railroad, 22, 34-35
Alaska Range, 29, 31, 36
Alaska, U.S. purchase of, 17-18
Alaskaland, 36
Aleut language, alphabet for, 45
Aleutian Islands/Chain, 16, 40-46; invasion of, 45
Aleutian Range, 41
Aleuts, 16, 41, 44-46; homes of, 44
Ambler, 58
Ambler River, 58
Anaktuvuk Pass, 59
Anchorage, 2-3, 4, 10, 21-24, 22-23, 34, 52
architecture, Russian, 14-15, 17, 24, 45, 53
Arctic, 7, 10-11, 54-59; climate, 55, 57; fauna, 55-59; flora, 58-59
Arctic Circle, 7, 38, 49, 51, 57
Arctic National Wildlife Refuge, 59
Arctic Ocean, 16, 59
Arctic Trades Fair, 58
Army (U.S.) bases, 22
Arrigetch Peaks, 59
Athapaskan Indians, 16, 24, 37, 49; beadwork of, 31, 37
Attu Island, invasion of, 45
aurora australis, 39

aurora borealis, 36, 39

baidarka, 44
bald eagle, 5, 16-17, 46
Baldwin Peninsula, 58
barabara, 44
Baranof Island, 18
Baronov, Alexander, 17
Barrow, 57-58
beadwork, Athapaskan, 31, 37
bears: *see* individual entries
Beaufort Sea, 57
Bering Island, 25
Bering Land Bridge National Preserve, 51
Bering Sea, 37, 41, 52
Bering Sea Coast: 46, 48-53; climate, 49, 51; fauna, 52-53; flora, 49, 51
Bering Sea Ice Golf Classic, 52
Bering Sea Land Bridge, 10
Bering, Vitus: expeditions of, 11, 16, 25, 45
Bethel, 52-53
Bettles, 59
Big Diomede Island, U.S.S.R., 51
birds, 7, 16, 23, 28-29, 34, 38, 43, 46, 52-53
Bristol Bay, 49, 51-53
British exploration/influence, 14, 21, 24
British fur trade/traders, 17, 38
Brooks Range, 6-7, 36, 57, 59
bush pilots, 23, 31

canneries, 46-47, 53
Cape Krusenstern National Monument, 59
caribou, 6-7, 11, 29, 34, 37, 52, 55, 58; Porcupine, 59
Chena Hot Springs, 37
Chena River, 34, 36
Chilkat Inlet, 18
Chilkat River Valley, 16
Chilkoot Inlet, 18
Chilkoot Pass/Trail, 18
Chitistone Canyon, 29
Chugach Mountains, 2-3, 4, 23
Chugach State Park, 23
Chukchi Sea, 43, 57-58
churches/cathedrals, Russian Orthodox: 24, 45, 53; Saint Michael's, 14-15, 17
Circle Hot Springs, 37
Cold Bay, 43
Cook Inlet, 21-22, 28-29
Cook, Captain James, 17, 21
Copper River, 28
Copper River Delta, 28
Cordova, 25, 28

Dall sheep, 29, 34
Dall, William, 38
Dawson Creek, B.C., 36
Delta Junction, 36
Denali National Park and Preserve, 34. *See also* Mount McKinley
Depression, Great, 24
Dillingham, 53
Diomede, 51
Discovery III, 36
Dot Lake, 36
dune fields, 37, 59
Dutch Harbor, 45
Dyea, 18

Eagle, 38
eagle, bald, 5, 16-17, 46
earthquake(s), 41; of 1964, 22, 28
Eklutna, 24
Ekuk, 53
emperor goose, 52-53
Eskimo spirit carvings, 6, 21
Eskimos, 24, 39, 44, 50-51, 55-59; masks of, 11, 55; and whale hunting, 58-59. *See also* Inupiat, Nunamiut, *and* Yupik Eskimos
European exploration/settlement, 38, 44-45, 57-58. *See also* British, Russian, *and* Spanish exploration

Fairbanks, 34, 36-37; Univ. of Alaska at, 36

fish, 16, 37-38, 43. *See also* individual entries
fishing, commercial, 28, 37, 41, 45-46, 49, 53
floatplanes, *58;* largest base for, *10, 23. See also* air taxi services *and* bush pilots
Fort Yukon, 38
Fortymile River, 38
fur seals, 44, 46
fur trade/traders: 10, 25; British, 17, 38; Russian, 16-17, 24-25, 38, 44-45

Galena, 37
Gambell, 51
Gates of the Arctic National Park and Preserve, *58-59*
Geophysical Institute (Univ. of Alaska), 36, 39
Glacier Bay, *19*
Glacier Bay National Park and Preserve, 19
glaciers: 7; in Southeast, 11, 13, 16, 18-19; Malaspina, 29; Mendenhall, *16,* 19
gold rushes: 18, 24, 38; Juneau, 14, 18; Klondike, 28; Nome, 46, 52
gold seekers, 10, 18, 25, 34, 36, 38
goose, emperor, 52-53
Great Kobuk Sand Dunes, 59
grizzly bear, 7, 27, 34, 52; coastal, 16, 43
Gulf Coast. *See* Southcentral/Gulf Coast
Gulf of Alaska, 28-29
Gull Island, 29

Haida Indians, 16
Haines, 18
halibut, *29*
Halibut Cove, 29
Harding, President Warren G., 34
Homer, 24, 29
Hoonah, 16
Hope, 24
Hudson's Bay Company, 17
hunting practices, Eskimo: 53, 55; whaling, 58-59
Hydaburg, 16

icebergs, *16*
Iditarod Trail Sled Dog Race, 52
Iguigig, 53
Iliamna, 53
Indians: Athapaskan, 16,

24, *31,* 37, 49; Haida, 16; Tanaina, 24, 31; Tlingit, *5, 13,* 16; Tsimshian, 16
Inside Passage, 13-14, 18
Interior, the: 31-39; climate, 36; flora/fauna, 34, 37-38
Inupiat Eskimos, 16, 49, 52, 55; homes of, *57;* hunting practices of, 55
Islands of the Four Mountains, 41
ivory, 46, 49, 51-52
Izembeck National Wildlife Refuge, 43

jade, 58
Jade Mountains, 58
Japanese Current, 41
Juneau, *13,* 16; gold rush, 14, 18
Juneau Ice Fields, 19

Kachemak Bay, 28-29
Kantishna River, 34
Katmai National Park and Preserve, 42-44
Kayak Island, 25
Kenai National Wildlife Refuge, 28
Kenai Peninsula, 21, 28-*29*
Kenai River, 28
Ketchikan, *5,* 14
Kiana, *51*
Kijik village, 53
killer whale (orca), 13, 17
King Island, 52
King Island Inupiat Singers and Dancers, 52
Kiska Island, invasion of, 45
Klawock, 16
Klondike gold rush, 28. *See also* gold rushes
Klondike Gold Rush National Historical Park, 18
Kluane National Park, Yukon Terr., 29
Knik Arm, 24
Kobuk, 57-58
Kobuk River, 58-59
Kobuk Valley National Park, 59
Kodiak, 45; seafood processing plant in, 46-47
Kodiak Island, 45
Kokhanok, 53, 58-59
Kotzebue, Otto von, 57
Koyukuk National Wildlife Refuge, 37
Koyukuk River, 37

Kuskokwim Bay, 52
Kuskokwim River, 34, 52

Lake Bennett, Yukon Terr., 18
Lake Clark, 53
Lake Clark National Park and Preserve, 53
Lake Hood, *10*
Lake Hood Air Harbor, 23
Levelock, 53
Little Diomede Island, 51
Little Norway Festival, 14
Lynn Canal, 18

Malaspina Glacier, 29
Mankjoitak, 53
marine mammals, 13, 43-44, 58
Matanuska Valley, 24, 36
McNeil River State Game Preserve, *26-27*
Mendenhall Glacier, *16,* 19
Merrill Field, 23
minerals/mining, 24, 49. *See also* gold rushes
moose, 7, 23-24, 28, 34, 37
Mount Eccles, 28
Mount Iliamna, 29
Mount McKinley, *5, 31-33,* 34, 38
Mount Redoubt, 29
Muir, John, 11; *Travels in Alaska* (quotes), 13, 19
muktuk, 59
musk-oxen, 52-53

Naknek Lake, 44
Native culture/peoples, 7, 11, 13-14, 16, 49, 58-59. *See also* Aleuts, Eskimos, *and* Indians
Nenana, 34
New Archangel (Sitka), 17
Nizina Canyon, 29
Noatak River, 57
Nome, *52;* gold rush, 46, 52
North Slope Borough, 58
northern lights, 11, 39. *See also* aurora borealis
Northwest Passage, 5
Nulato, 38
Nunamiut Eskimos, 59
Nunivak Island, 49, 52

oil industry, 22, 28, 57-58
oil spill, Prince William Sound, 28
Old Ninilchik, 29

Pacific Northwest Coast, 13
Pacific Ocean, 41, 43
Palmer, 24

Panhandle, 14. *See also* Southeast Alaska
Petersburg, 14
Peterson Bay, 29
pingo, 57
pipeline, trans-Alaska, 22, 28, 57
Point Hope, 55, 58-59
polar bear, 7, 10, *55-56*, 58-59
Porcupine River, 37
Port Alsworth, 53
Port Franklin, 43
potlatch, Tlingit, 16
Pribilof Islands, 41-42, 45-46
Prince William Sound, 21, 28; oil spill, 28
promyshlenniki, Russian, 44-45
Prudhoe Bay, 57
puffin, tufted, 16, 29, *43*, 46
Puget Sound, 16

qiviut, 53

Rampart, 37
Ring of Fire, 41
River Lethe Gorge, *43-44*
Roosevelt, President Theodore, 14
Ruby, 37
Russian architecture, *14-15*, 17, 24, 45, 53
Russian exploration/ influence, 14, 16-17, 24-25, 28-29, 44-45, 53; and Tanaina Indians, 24
Russian fur trade/traders, 16-17, 24-25, 38, 44-45
Russian Orthodox churches/cathedrals: 24, 45, 53; Saint Michael's, *14-15*, 17
Russian-American Company, 17, 46

Saint Michael's Cathedral, *14-15*, 17
salmon, 7, 16, 23, 28, 37-38, 46, *51-52*, 53
sand dunes, 37, 59
Sand Point, 46
Savage River Canyon, 34
Savoonga, 51
sea cow, 25, 45-46
sea otter, 44, 46
sea otter pelts, trade of, 16-17, 25, 45
seafood processing, 45-46, 47
Seattle, Washington, 13
Seldovia, 28

seracs, 11
Seward, 24, 34
Seward Peninsula, 49, 51-52
Sheldon Jackson College and Museum, 17
Shemya Island, Air Force base on, 45
Ship Creek, 23
Shishmaref, 52
Shumagin Islands, 46
Shungnak, 58
Sitka, *14*, 17
Sitka National Historic Fort, 17
Skagway, 13, 18
sled dog racing, *52*
Southcentral/Gulf Coast: 20-29; climate, 21; flora/fauna, 28-29
Southeast: 12-19; climate of, 14; flora/fauna of, 14, 16; glaciers of, 11, 13, *16*, 18-19
Spanish exploration, 24
spirit houses, 24
St. George Island, 46
St. Lawrence Island, 49, 51
St. Paul, 46
St. Paul Island, 46
Steller eider, 25, 43, 53
Steller, Georg Wilhelm, 11, 25, 45
Steller jay, 25
Steller sea lion, 13, 25
stern trawler, Soviet, 46
Stikine River, 14, 18

taiga, 37
Talkeetna, 31
Tanaina Indians, 31; and Russian influence, 24
Tanalian Falls, 53
Tanana River, 34, 36-37
Tanana River valley, 34, 36
Teller, 52
Tetlin Wildlife Refuge, 29
Tikchik River, 53
Tlingit Indians, 16; community house, 5; and potlatch, 16; totem poles of, 13
Togiak National Wildlife Refuge, 53
Togiak River, 53
Tok, 36
Tongass National Forest, 14
Totem Heritage Center, 14
totem poles, *13-14*
traders. *See* fur trade/traders
trans-Alaska pipeline, 22, 28, 57

Tsimshian Indians, 16
tundra, 6-7, 10, 37, 43, 51-52
Turnagain Arm, 21, 24

Ukivok, 52
ulu, 50-51
umiaks, 55
Unalaska, 45-46
Unalaska Island, 45
University of Alaska, Fairbanks, 36, 39
Upper Koyukuk River, 59

Valdez, 24, 28, 57
Valley of Ten Thousand Smokes, 43-44
Vancouver, George, 19
volcanoes, 29, 41-42, 51; Novarupta, 43

walrus, 1, 4, 53, 55
Wasilla, 24
Western Union Telegraph Expedition, 38
whale hunting, 51, 55, 58-59
whale, orca, 13, *17*
whales, 7, 13-14, *17*, 43
White Pass & Yukon Route, 18
White Pass, B.C.
Whitehorse, Yukon Territory, 18
Whittier, 28
William Egan Convention Center, *21*
Windham Bay, 18
wolf, 7, 23, *37*, 52
Wonder Lake, *5*, 34
Wood-Tikchik State Park, 53
World War II, 36, 45, 51
Wrangell, 14
Wrangell-St. Elias National Park and Preserve, 29
Wrangell-St. Elias Range, 29

Yakutat Bay, 16
Yukon Delta National Wildlife Refuge, 52
Yukon River, 37-38, 52
Yukon-Charley Rivers National Preserve, 38
Yukon-Kuskokwim Delta, 51-53
Yupik Eskimos, 16, 49, 51-53; dialect of, 53; hunting code of, 53

ALASKA NORTHWEST BOOKS™

offers many more intriguing books about the North Country, including: The MILEPOST®, The ALASKA WILDERNESS MILEPOST®, and NORTHWEST MILEPOSTS®.

Ask for these books at your favorite bookstore, or contact **Alaska Northwest Books**™ *for a catalog of our entire selection.*

Since 1949, *The MILEPOST®* has served as the bible of North Country travel. Updated annually, this classic guide provides mile-by-mile information on what to see and do, and where to find food, gas, and lodging. It includes a fold-out "Plan-a-Trip" map and information on customs, air travel, state ferries, fishing, and more. Companion guides, *The ALASKA WILDERNESS MILEPOST®* (with facts about over 250 remote towns and villages in Alaska), and *NORTHWEST MILEPOSTS®* (covering Washington, Oregon, Idaho, western Montana, and southwestern Canada), round out the picture. With countless photos and maps.

The MILEPOST®/600 pages/softbound/$16.95 ($18.95 Canadian)/ISBN 088240-215-3

The ALASKA WILDERNESS MILEPOST®/480 pages/softbound/$14.95 ($18.95 Canadian)/ISBN 0-88240-290-0

NORTHWEST MILEPOSTS®/328 pages/softbound/$14.95 ($18.95 Canadian)/ISBN 0-88240-278-1

Facts About Alaska: THE ALASKA ALMANAC®, Fifteenth Edition.
Whether the subject is popular—the Iditarod Trail Sled Dog Race, for instance—or matter of fact, you'll find the latest information, drawings, and maps to answer any question about America's Last Frontier, Alaska. With 60 drawings, 20 maps.
232 pages/softbound/$8.95 ($10.95 Canadian)/ISBN 0-88240-248-X

To the Top of Denali: Climbing Adventures on North America's Highest Peak, by Bill Sherwonit.
This comprehensive collection of Mount McKinley climbing stories will enthrall any lover of adventure tales. Gripping narratives recount the challenges, triumphs, and tragedies of climbing North America's highest peak. With 29 photographs and 2 maps.
368 pages/softbound/$10.95 ($13.95 Canadian)/ISBN 0-88240-402-4

Along the Alaska Highway, photography by Alissa Crandall, text by Gloria J. Maschmeyer.
From Dawson Creek, British Columbia, to Delta Junction, Alaska, the Alaska Highway forges a 1,500-mile path through dense forest and raw wilderness. Award winners Alissa Crandall and Gloria J. Maschmeyer use spectacular full-color images and engaging text to reveal the people and landscape of the highway in all its seasons. If you are planning a trip along this historic roadway or simply dreaming about one, the book is an enticing call to adventure.
96 pages/softbound/$16.95 ($20.95 Canadian)/ISBN 0-88240-410-5

Alaska Northwest Books™
a division of GTE Discovery Publications
P.O. Box 3007, Bothell, WA 98041-3007
(800) 343-4567